COLORING BOOKS FOR EVERYONE

MW00597635

Thank you for purchasing our coloring book!

We hope you have a fun and relaxing experience when coloring.

Everyone who worked on this book appreciates your support.

STUFFED ANIMALS BY JADE SUMMER

STUFFED ANIMALS BY JADE SUMMER

STUFFED ANIMALS BY JADE SUMMER

STUFFED ANIMALS BY JADE SUMMER

STUFFED ANIMALS BY JADE SUMMER

We have included a second copy of each image.

You can color your favorite images a second time, have an extra copy in case you make a mistake, or share one of our pages with a friend.

We hope this makes your coloring experience even better.

STUFFED ANIMALS BY JADE SUMMER

STUFFED ANIMALS BY JADE SUMMER

STUFFED ANIMALS BY JADE SUMMER

NOTES

This page is for testing and documenting your color choices.

Made in the USA
Coppell, TX
19 May 2024